Physical Fitness

Dr. Alvin Silverstein,

Virginia Silverstein, and

Laura Silverstein Nunn

My Health

Franklin Watts

A Division of Scholastic Inc.

New York • Toronto • London • Auckland • Sydney

Mexico City • New Delhi • Hong Kong

Danbury, Connecticut

Photographs © 2001: Corbis-Bettmann: 29 (Jennie Woodcock/Reflections Photolibrary), 5 (Michael S. Yamashita); Envision/Steven Needham: 27; Photo Researchers, NY: 11 right (Gary Carlson), 21 (Tim Davis), 8 (David Gifford/SPL), 24 (Margot Granitsas), 11 left, 12 (Carlyn Iverson), 34 (Doug Martin), 17 (Lawrence Migdale), 23 (Sylvie Villeger/Explorer); PhotoEdit: 26 (Cindy Charles), 14 right (Cassy Cohen), 14 left (Gary A. Connor), 15 bottom (Myrleen Ferguson), 6 (Bonnie Kamin), 4, 15 top, 16, 35 (Michael Newman), 18 (David Young-Wolff); Visuals Unlimited: 9, 31, 38 (Mark E. Gibson), 37 (E. Webber).

Cartoons by Rick Stromoski

Library of Congress Cataloging-in-Publication Data

Silverstein, Alvin.
  Physical fitness / by Alvin Silverstein, Virginia Silverstein, and Laura Silverstein Nunn.
      p. cm.—(My Health)
    Includes bibliographical references and index.
    ISBN 0-531-11860-6 (lib. bdg.)   0-531-15563-3 (pbk.)
    1. Physical fitness—Juvenile literature. Physical fitness for children—Juvenile literature [1. Physical fitness.] I. Silverstein, Virginia B. II. Nunn, Laura Silverstein III. Title IV. Series
RA777.S5184   2002
613.7—dc21   2001017577

Contents

Fit for Life

How do you feel when you hear the word *exercise*? You probably think, "Yuck! That sounds like a lot of work!" But did you know you actually exercise every single day? Every time you move, you are exercising your body—when you climb stairs, play on the jungle gym, walk the dog, or run around during soccer practice. All of these activities help to keep your body physically fit.

What does it mean to be physically fit? Fitness is a combination of several different things. Can you carry a heavy box up a flight of stairs? To lift the box, your body needs to be **flexible** so you can bend and twist. You need to be strong, too, to pick up the box and carry it without dropping it. You also need to have **endurance** (staying power) to

This girl is getting a lot of exercise by playing with her dog.
▼

◀ Everyday activities, like carrying a box up a flight of stairs, exercise your body.

keep moving up the stairs without getting tired. You need balance to keep from falling over. All these things—flexibility, strength, endurance, and balance—are part of physical fitness.

Being active helps to keep you physically fit. But some people are more active than others. Some kids may spend hours watching television or playing video games. They hardly move their bodies at all. Others, however, get a good workout when they go for bike rides, shoot hoops, jump rope, or play ball with their friends.

Everybody needs to exercise, especially kids. Your body is still growing and exercise helps to keep it strong, healthy, and flexible. It also makes you feel really good.

Recess is important because it is a time for you to get some exercise.

Exercising is only part of becoming physically fit. How you feel also depends on the kind of foods you eat and how much sleep you get. If you build a strong, healthy body and good habits when you are young, you are more likely to stay fit all through your life.

Are you physically fit? What can you do to keep your body in shape and feel better? Read on to find out.

Did You Know...

The best time to start exercising is now while you're young. Kids who exercise regularly develop the habit of being active and are more likely to stay active when they get older.

Your Body Is a Machine

Every move you make, from picking up a pencil to taking a giant leap, involves a combined effort of many different parts of your body. The hard, strong bones inside you give your body support. The bones are connected to each other at **joints** and are tied together by strong straps called **ligaments**. The ligaments help to keep the bones from slipping out of place.

Your bones can't move without **muscles**. Muscles are like strong rubber bands that can stretch and **contract** (get shorter). The muscles are attached to the bones by tough cords called **tendons**. When the muscle contracts, it pulls on the bones and makes your body move.

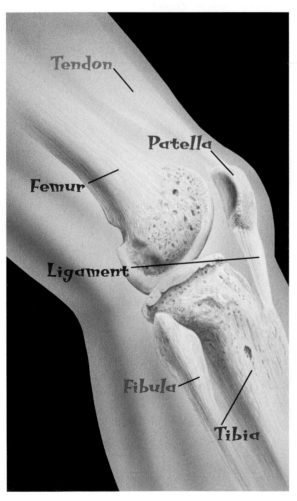

Tendon

Patella

Femur

Ligament

Fibula

Tibia

The Knee

8

Muscles usually work together in pairs. They can only pull—they cannot push. When you bend your arm to make a muscle, for example, the big muscle on the front of your upper arm (biceps) contracts. When you straighten your arm out, the biceps relaxes and the muscle on the back of your upper arm (triceps) contracts.

Muscles need energy to do the work of moving your body. They get this energy from the foods you eat. Inside the muscles, food chemicals are burned in

Fun Facts about Muscles

There are over 640 muscles in your body. They allow you to make many different kinds of movements, from the tiny muscles in your face that let you smile or frown, to the large muscles in your legs that let you run or jump.

For each movement, you use dozens of muscles. When you speak, you use about 72 different muscles. To move your foot, 13 leg muscles and 20 foot muscles are needed. You use about 17 muscles to smile and 43 muscles to frown!

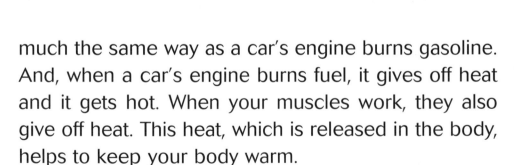

much the same way as a car's engine burns gasoline. And, when a car's engine burns fuel, it gives off heat and it gets hot. When your muscles work, they also give off heat. This heat, which is released in the body, helps to keep your body warm.

Your body needs oxygen to release the energy stored in food. Oxygen is an invisible gas that is part of the air. When you breathe, air comes in through your nose and mouth and passes down into two large, spongy organs called **lungs**. They contain many tiny air bags, each of which is too small to see with your eyes alone. Oxygen passes out of these tiny air bags into the blood.

Blood carries both oxygen and food chemicals. Your heart is a pump that sends blood rushing through a network of tubes, the **blood vessels**, to nourish the body cells. The blood also carries away the cells' waste products. The heart and blood vessels together make up the **cardiovascular system** (*cardio* means heart).

Your heart is actually a muscle. The pumping action occurs when the heart muscle contracts. Before each contraction, the heart fills with blood. Blood from all over your body flows into the right side of the heart, while oxygen-rich blood from the

When you breathe, air travels in and out of your lungs.

Lungs

Diaphragm

These are highly magnified blood vessels from the lungs.

11

lungs flows into the left side. Then, when the heart contracts, the right side sends blood to the lungs to get a new supply of oxygen. The left side pumps the oxygen-rich blood from the lungs into a big blood vessel whose branches lead to all parts of the body.

The Heart

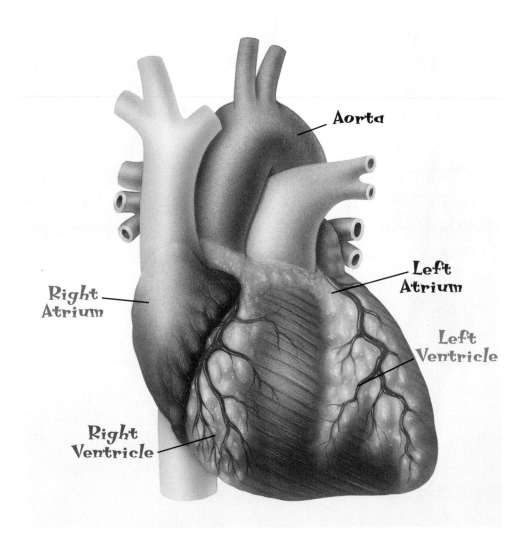

Aorta

Right Atrium

Left Atrium

Left Ventricle

Right Ventricle

Each contraction of your heart is called a **heartbeat**. You can hear the heartbeat if you put your ear to somebody else's chest. When the heart beats, you will hear two sounds—a long "lub" sound, quickly followed by a shorter "dub" sound. These sounds are made when little trap doors inside the heart snap shut to keep the blood from flowing backward.

All the actions performed by your body are controlled by the brain and nerves, which keep everything working together smoothly.

When you get your body moving, all the parts of your body are affected. How you work your muscles, how often you use them, and the kind of fuel you use to power them, will determine how well your body machine will run.

Get Physical

Are you a couch potato? Do you spend hours glued to the television or playing video games? To be healthy and fit, you need to be active—you need to move your body. But how can you do that if you are sitting on the couch all the time?

Too Much TV

Kids today are not as active as were the kids of the past. Many kids spend more time watching TV, playing video games, or using the computer than they spend getting involved in outdoor activities. The average child in the United States watches 28 hours of television per week. That adds up to two straight months of TV-watching every year!

To be physically fit, you need to be active and exercise. You should watch television and play video games in moderation.

Exercise is a great way to get physically fit. When you work your muscles, your body goes through some amazing changes. Try this: If you run in place for a few minutes and then stop, you'll notice that your breathing is heavier than usual and your heart feels like it's pounding harder in your chest. Your heart rate can more than double during exercise. During exercise, the muscles are working hard, and they need more energy—which means they need more oxygen too. So you need to breathe faster and deeper to take in enough oxygen to meet your active body's needs. Your heart also needs to pump the oxygen-rich blood faster than normal to provide the muscles with extra energy.

You don't have to go out and jog or do a hundred jumping jacks to get your body into shape. Exercise can be any activity that you like to do, such as bike riding, swimming, playing basketball, dancing, or playing soccer. These kinds of activities are considered **aerobic**,

These children are staying active.

Exercise!!!!

Health experts say that you have to exercise for at least twenty minutes without stopping to get all of its health benefits.

which means "needing oxygen." Aerobic exercise is any kind of activity that uses oxygen to power the muscles and works the lungs and heart.

To stay physically fit, you need to exercise regularly—at least three times a week. Exercise helps to increase your cardiovascular fitness in several different ways. An aerobic "cardio" workout makes the heart stronger and can even make it bigger. So if you exercise regularly, your heart can pump more blood in each beat. You also produce more red

Sometimes it is easier to keep up an exercise routine if you exercise with someone.

blood cells, which pick up and carry oxygen to the body cells. So each drop of your blood can carry even more oxygen than it could if you didn't exercise. The blood can move more easily through your blood vessels too.

All of the changes that result from exercise make your heart beat more slowly because it doesn't have to pump as much to get enough blood to the body. An athlete's heart can beat as slow as fifty times a minute during rest. Compare this to the average child's heart, which beats about eighty times a minute, and an adult with a heart rate of seventy to eighty beats per minute.

How can you tell how fast your heart is beating? Doctors listen to the heartbeat with an instrument called a **stethoscope**. It magnifies the heart sounds so they can be heard outside the body. But there are easier ways to find out how fast your heart is beating. Each heartbeat sends blood rushing out through large blood vessels called **arteries**. As the blood passes through them, muscles in the artery

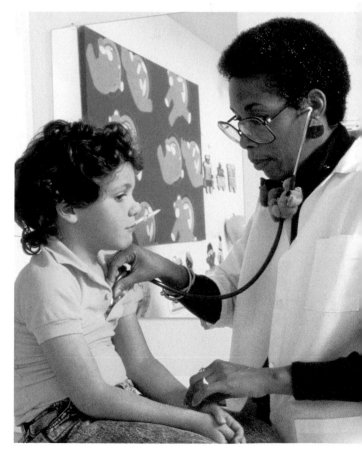

This doctor is listening to her patient's heart.

walls contract to help send the blood along. You can feel these contractions with your fingertips in places where arteries are close to the surface of the skin. The throbbing that you feel is called the **pulse**, and it has the same rate as your heartbeat. The most common places to take your pulse are in the inner side of the wrists and the sides of the neck.

The throbbing you feel on your wrists is your pulse.

Activity 1:
Check Your Pulse

You can get an idea of how physically fit you are by taking your pulse before and after you exercise. Before you exercise, place the three middle fingers of one hand on the inside of your other wrist (on the side by the thumb) and press gently until you feel a regular throbbing. Look at the second hand of a clock or watch. Count the number of beats in your wrist for fifteen seconds. Multiply the number of beats you have counted by four and write it down. That is your resting pulse rate. (You can also check your pulse rate by putting two fingers on the side of your neck just under the jaw bone.)

Then step up and down on a stair, moving one foot after the other. Keep doing this for three minutes. When the time is up, immediately take your pulse again and write it down. This is your exercise pulse rate. Compare the two readings.

You can measure how your pulse rate will improve if you start exercising regularly. An unfit person may have an exercise pulse rate between 140 and 160 beats per minute. But a fit person may be around 100 to 110 beats per minute.

What about lifting weights? Weight training is not an aerobic exercise, but it can help to make your muscles stronger. There's a danger, though, if you lift weights while you are still growing. Lifting very heavy weights can damage the growth centers inside your bones. Then you might not grow as tall as you should. Doctors today believe that a little weight training can be good for kids, but they should never work out this way alone. Weight training is something kids should do only under the supervision of an adult who knows all about the benefits and dangers of this kind of exercise.

When you lift heavy objects or exercise, your bones get stronger and thicker. Your muscles also become stronger. The more you use your muscles, the stronger they get. Stronger muscles allow you to do activities for longer periods of time, so your endurance increases. For instance, say you used to get tired

Are You Tired Yet?

Why do you feel tired after doing an activity for a while? When you work your muscles for long periods of time, they become overworked and chemicals in your body make them tired. You can see this for yourself by making a fist and then opening it. Do this as fast as you can and as many times as you can. Soon you will have to stop because your muscles will get tired. The more you exercise, however, the longer you can go without getting tired.

after bike riding for only fifteen minutes. But you've been riding your bike much more often for the past month or so—and now you can ride your bike for forty-five minutes without getting too tired.

Exercise also helps to protect you from getting hurt. Your strong bones are less likely to break. And stronger muscles give better support to joints. Your tendons and ligaments get stronger too. Exercise also makes your body more flexible—you can move and bend better. Before and after you exercise, however, you should always stretch. Stretching helps to warm up and loosen your muscles so that they can

These girls are stretching before soccer practice. It is important to stretch your muscles before and after exercise.

contract better. If you exercise without stretching, you may strain your muscles and wake up the next day with an aching body. Stretching after exercise helps your muscles "cool down" and keeps them from getting stiff.

Exercise also puts you in a better mood. When you exercise, your body makes special chemicals called **endorphins** that work in your brain to make you feel happy. The more you exercise, the more endorphins your body makes.

Exercise can also make you feel good about yourself. When you are stronger and you can do things better, you feel proud. So if you exercise, you will feel good all over.

Did You Know

Swimming is one the best types of exercise you can do. It helps you to improve your flexibility, strength, and endurance. You are also less likely to strain your muscles because your body is supported by the water.

Fuel Up for Fitness

Your body can't run without energy. You get this energy from the foods you eat. So how you feel depends a great deal on what you eat. A balanced diet that includes a variety of healthy foods will help you grow strong and stay healthy.

Don't Skip Breakfast!

Breakfast is the most important meal of the day. When you go to sleep at night, you spend many hours without eating. So when you wake up in the morning, you are low on energy. A good, healthy breakfast gives you the energy you need to start the day and keeps you going all morning. According to experts, children who eat a healthy breakfast do better in school than those who skip breakfast.

Toast, cereal, fruits, juice, and milk are all part of a healthy breakfast.

Meat, eggs, cheese, milk, fish, and poultry are all good sources of protein.

Potato chips and chocolate bars may be great tasting foods that give you a boost of energy, but they don't contain all the **nutrients** that your body needs. Important nutrients include **carbohydrates, proteins, fats, vitamins,** and **minerals.** Each kind of nutrient works differently in your body.

Carbohydrates are your body's main source of energy. Starchy foods, such as bread, pasta, potatoes, and rice, usually contain carbohydrates and many other important nutrients. Sugary foods, such as soda and candy also contain carbohydrates, but have very few other nutrients. Carbohydrates are broken down inside the body into a simple sugar called *glucose.* Glucose is the fuel used by the cells in your body.

Proteins give you energy, but they do other important things too. The proteins in meat, cheese, eggs, fish, and nuts help to build bones, hair, muscles, skin, and also to replace worn-out cells. The proteins in foods are also turned into chemicals that help control the many different reactions that go on inside the body when you move, breathe, digest your food, and even think.

Fats are found in butter, cheese, margarine, oil, and meat. Too much fat is not good for you, but you do need some in your diet. Like carbohydrates, fats are broken down and used for energy. They are also used to protect your body organs, to keep you warm, and to build nerves that carry messages from one part of your body to another.

Your body also needs small amounts of vitamins and minerals every day. Vitamins help turn other nutrients into energy. They also help build bones, body tissues, blood cells, and help protect you from diseases. Some important vitamins we should have in our diet are vitamins A, B, C, D, E, and K.

Like vitamins, minerals help build bones, blood cells, and teeth. Some important minerals are calcium, phosphorus, and iron. Nearly everyone loves the taste of salt, which contains the minerals sodium and chloride.

Water is one of the most important nutrients in your body. It makes up about 70 percent of your weight and is needed for many of the chemical reactions that take place inside you. You drink only about half of the water you need. The rest comes from the foods you eat, such as fruits and vegetables.

It is important to start drinking water even before you start to feel really thirsty or dehydrated.

Keep Drinking Water!

You lose water every time you sweat or go to the bathroom. You lose the most water by sweating during exercise and in hot weather. So you have to drink lots of water to replace the water that is lost, even if you don't feel thirsty.

It can be tough to make healthy food choices, but a ***food guide pyramid*** can help. A food guide pyramid shows you the kinds and amounts of food you need to eat every day. The foods in the pyramid are grouped according to the nutrients they provide.

This food guide pyramid shows the kinds and amounts of food you need each day.

You should eat a lot of the foods shown at the bottom of the pyramid. These include bread, cereal, rice, and pasta. You need a lot of fruits and vegetables too. Milk, yogurt, cheese, meat, poultry, fish, eggs, and nuts are higher up on the pyramid. These are good foods, but you should not eat too much of them.

Fats, oils, and sweets are at the top of the pyramid. You don't need much of these foods to stay healthy, but you may like to eat them because they taste good. It's okay to eat cakes, cookies, and ice cream once in a while, but you shouldn't eat them instead of other foods in the pyramid. Sweets will give you energy and some nutrients, but eating too many sweets can make you overweight. Eating a variety of good foods will help your body be the best that it can be.

Do You Think You're Fat?

When you think of physically fit people, do you picture those good-looking, skinny models you see on magazine covers? Or do you think of men and women with huge, bulging muscles? Do you hope that you can look like either type someday? If you do, you shouldn't.

Some kids think they are fat because they don't look like the people they see in magazines, on television, or in the movies. Others think they're too skinny because they don't have muscles like a champion

You don't need to look like the models in the magazines.

body builder. The truth is, *most* people do not look like models or sports stars.

To be physically fit, you need to maintain a healthy weight. Some kids worry so much about getting fat that they **diet** to lose weight. Medical experts worry that when young people diet, they may not be getting some important nutrients that their bodies need to grow.

Some kids develop really dangerous eating habits. **Anorexia nervosa** is a problem for some young people. People who suffer from this eating problem will actually starve themselves to become thin. **Bulimia** is another dangerous eating problem. People who are bulimic will eat as much as they can and then throw up so they won't gain weight.

People who eat more food than their bodies need may become overweight. Too much of any food can cause a weight problem. What your body does not use, it stores as fat. People who are seriously overweight are called **obese**. Millions of children in the United States are obese.

Carrying around a lot of extra fat puts a strain on the body. As a result, obese people often feel tired. They are also more likely than other people to develop serious health problems, such as cancer, diabetes, and heart disease.

How do you get rid of the extra pounds? The best way to lose weight is to eat a balanced diet and to cut down on the total amount of food you eat. You don't have to stop eating the foods you like. Just eat less of them. At the same time, you should exercise more. When you exercise, you burn **calories**. A calorie is a measurement of the amount of energy that food gives you. This energy comes from carbohydrates, proteins, and fats. One gram of protein or carbohydrate contains about four calories of energy. One gram of fat contains about nine calories.

The more you exercise, the more calories you burn. Hiking is great exercise!

How many calories do you need to eat every day? That depends on how old you are, how large your body is, and whether you are a boy or a girl. It also depends on how active you are. Do you play a lot of sports or do you spend a lot of time sitting down watching television? The more active you are, the more energy you use and the more calories your body requires. The average child needs about 2,300 calories a day to be healthy.

Did You Know....

An average chocolate bar has 270 calories. To burn off the calories from one chocolate bar, you need to run for fourteen minutes, walk for fifty-two minutes, or swim for twenty-four minutes.

How well you burn calories depends on your **metabolism**. Scientists use the word metabolism to describe all the chemical reactions that take place inside your body. These chemical reactions build and repair the cells in your blood, muscles, nerves, and other body tissues. Exercise helps to speed up your metabolism. The faster your metabolism, the better your body is at burning calories and losing weight.

Do You Get Enough Sleep?

Do you feel like you're dragging during much of the day? Do you have trouble keeping your eyes open in class? If this happens to you, you may not be getting enough sleep.

During the day you use up a lot of energy by thinking, moving, and eating. By the end of the day, you are tired. You need to sleep so your body can rest. Sleep is very important. While you are asleep, your body can heal cuts, bruises, and sore muscles. A good night's sleep also helps you grow, regain your strength, and think clearly.

Did You Know...

Children from six to twelve years old need an average of ten to twelve hours of sleep.

You can tell when you haven't gotten a good night's sleep. You still feel tired when you wake up. You may be in a bad mood all day. Your body feels like it is dragging. This is your body's way of saying, "I need sleep!" Lack of sleep keeps your body and mind from working properly.

If you don't get the right amount of sleep, you may find it hard to think, concentrate, and remember things. Making a simple decision like choosing what to eat for lunch may seem difficult. You may slur your words when you try to talk, or say things you don't mean. Things you write or draw may look sloppy, and you may be clumsy when you run and jump. All of these problems may lead to trouble with schoolwork.

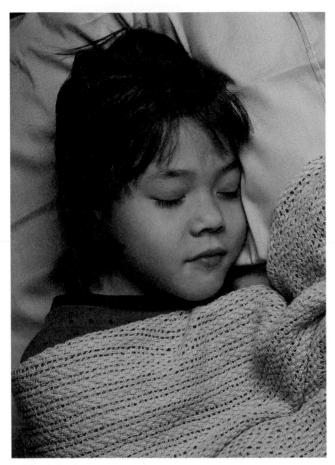

The amount of sleep you get each night can have an effect on how you do in school. If you are tired, you may not pay attention as much as you should.

Missing sleep can ruin your mood too. You may be very moody, irritable, depressed, or anxious. And, if you don't get enough sleep, you are more likely to get sick. A lack of sleep weakens your body's defenses, which makes it harder to fight off disease germs.

If you have trouble getting enough sleep, you need to develop good sleeping habits. Going to bed and getting up at the same time each day can help you feel ready to go to sleep quickly at night. A bedtime routine can help too. Brushing your teeth, putting on your pajamas, and listening to soft music or reading a book in bed for a little while can help to put you in the mood for sleep when you do them every night.

Having someone read to you before you go to bed can be a part of your bedtime routine.

Good eating habits can also help you sleep well. Eating too much candy or drinking a lot of cola drinks can keep you feeling wide awake for hours. Eating a big meal late in the day can also make it hard to fall asleep. Drinking a glass of warm milk at bedtime is a good idea. The warmth is soothing and relaxing, and milk contains a chemical that the body uses to make you feel sleepy.

Could exercising help you get to sleep? Not if you do it right before bedtime. A good workout gets your heart pumping faster and makes you feel energetic and wide awake. But regular exercise during the day can help to relieve stress and tension that could keep you awake at night.

Getting enough sleep gives you the energy you need to make it through the day and feel good doing all that you do.

Did You Know...

Studies show that people who get enough sleep are healthier than those with poor sleeping habits. They live longer too.

Fitting Fitness into Your Life

If you're visiting a friend who lives a few blocks away, do you walk or do you have someone drive you? Would you rather spend a warm, sunny afternoon playing video games or getting a group of friends together and playing kickball?

You make choices like these every single day. What you decide will determine how physically fit you will be. Doing things the active way instead of being a couch potato can help you get and stay fit. You can even get active while you are reading a book or watching TV. Don't just sit still; kick your legs or stretch your shoulders or pump your arms. (Do things like that when you are alone, not in the classroom!)

Gymnastics is a wonderful sport for keeping fit and flexible.

Working some kind of regular exercise into your daily routine is a good idea too. Starting an exercise program can be a lot of fun, but sticking to it can be a lot tougher. There are many things that you can do to make exercise fun.

Make sure the exercise is something you like to do. It can be anything that gets your heart pumping: bike riding, playing kickball, dancing, playing basketball, or roller skating. Keep it interesting so you don't get bored. Change the activity to keep your mind alert and to challenge your body.

This family is exercising together. Do you spend time exercising with your family?

Exercise with a friend or a family member. Working out with somebody else is a lot more fun than doing it alone. Also, you're more likely to stay motivated when you have somebody else rooting for you.

Realize that becoming physically fit is a gradual process. You will not become physically fit overnight—it takes time. If you keep a fitness diary to chart your progress, you can look back each week and see how far you have come. For instance, right now you may get tired after exercising for only ten minutes. But maybe next week you'll be up to fifteen or twenty minutes.

Give yourself goals so you can work toward them. For example, if you can walk a mile before you get tired, aim at walking an extra tenth of a mile before you stop to rest. Don't be too hard on yourself if you don't quite make your goal as soon as you expected. Your body may just need a little more time to adjust to the work.

The more you exercise, the easier it will get for you, as your body gets used to working out. After a while, you'll find that exercise and physical fitness will be a part of your life—something you can't wait to do and feel good doing.

Activity 2: How Fit Are Your Friends?

Here are some questions to ask your friends and relatives to find out how fit they are.

1. Do you have trouble catching your breath after you walk up a flight of stairs?

2. What is your pulse rate when you are sitting down and resting? What is your pulse rate after you have been running or going up and down stairs?

3. How far can you walk or run before you get tired?

4. Can you pick up a heavy bag of groceries and carry it?

5. How many flights of stairs do you go up and down each day? Do you take the elevator or escalator instead of the stairs?

7. Do you walk to work or school, or do you drive? How far is it?

8. Do you ride a bike? How often? How far?

9. Do you exercise or play sports regularly? How often? What do you do?

10. Do you eat breakfast? Do you try to eat foods from all of the food groups?

11. How much sleep do you get each night?

12. How tall are you? How much do you weigh? Do you think you're overweight? How fit do you think you are?

Glossary

aerobic exercise—any activity that uses oxygen to power muscles and works the heart and lungs

anorexia nervosa—an eating problem in which a person is obsessed with being thin and refuses to eat enough food to stay healthy

artery (arteries pl.)—a blood vessel that carries blood away from the heart to any part of the body

blood vessel—a tube that carries blood from one part of the body to another

bulimia—an eating problem in which a person overeats and then throws up to get rid of the excess food

calorie—a measurement of the amount of energy that food gives you

carbohydrate—a starch or sugar; a nutrient that provides the body with energy

cardiovascular system—the heart and blood vessels

contract—to shorten

dieting—eating reduced amounts of food or certain kinds of food, to lose weight

endorphins—chemicals released in the body that send "happy messages" to the brain

endurance—ability to continue an activity without getting tired

fat—a high-energy nutrient; the main energy store of the body

flexibility—the ability to bend and twist

food guide pyramid—a diagram showing the kinds and amounts of foods that make up a balanced diet

glucose—a simple sugar used as fuel by body cells

heartbeat—the rhythmic sounds made as the heart contracts and pumps blood

joints—connections between bones, such as elbows and knees

ligaments—tough bands of tissue wrapped around joints that hold bones together

lungs—two baglike organs used for breathing

metabolism—all the chemical reactions that go on in the body

mineral—a chemical in foods that is used to build blood cells, bones, and teeth. Calcium, phosphorus, and iron are minerals.

muscles—strong, elastic tissues that pull on bones or other structures and move body parts

nutrient—a chemical in food that is used by the body

obese—seriously overweight

protein—a nutrient that provides energy and helps build and repair bones, hair, muscles, and skin

pulse—the regular throbbing of the arteries in time with the contractions of the heart

stethoscope—a medical instrument that magnifies the heart sounds so they can be heard outside the body

tendons—tough bands of tissue that connect muscles to bones

vitamin—an essential nutrient found in small amounts in foods. Vitamins take part in various chemical reactions to keep the body healthy.

Learning More

Books

A Child's First Library of Learning: Health & Safety. Alexandria: Time-Life Books, 1996.

Cooper, Kenneth H. *Fit Kids! The Complete Shape-Up Program from Birth through High School*. Nashville: Broadman & Holman Publishers, 1999.

Laderer, Mandy. *Fit Kids: Getting Kids "Hooked" on Fitness Fun*. Hicksville: Allure Publishing, 1993.

Landy, Joanne and Keith Burridge. *50 Simple Things You Can Do to Raise a Child Who Is Physically Fit*. New York: Simon & Schuster Macmillan Company, 1997.

Pamphlets

American Institute for Cancer Research, "A Healthy Weight for Life," 1998.

American Institute for Cancer Research, "Getting Active, Staying Active: How to Enjoy a More Physically Active Life," 1999.

Online Sites
Physical Activity
http://www.americanheart.org/Health/Lifestyle/Physical_Activity/
This internet site is provided by the American Heart Association. It includes links to lots of interesting and helpful information about physical activity and staying healthy.

Physical Fitness
http://kidshealth.org/kid
This site is provided by KidsHealth.org. You can find lots of information about fitness by typing in the keyword "fitness" and clicking on "Search." You will get pages of links about fitness, including exercise, nutrition, and other information about your health.

Fitness For Kids
http://home.earthlink.net/~svanhorn/rthf.html
This site is full of colorful, animated graphics accompanied by a rap tune soundtrack about exercise. There are lots of links to information about sports and other fun activities. Fun facts and a puzzle page add to the kid-friendly format.

Healthy Eating and Physical Activity
http://www.ific.org/proactive/newsroom/release.vtml?id=18321
This site, provided by the International Food Information Council Foundation, has 10 tips to help you eat right and stay active.

Get Up Get Out
http://fitness.gov
This is the official website of the President's Council on Physical Fitness and Sports. It provides exercise, physical activity, and health information, plus tips for "funfit kids."

Index

Page numbers in *italics* indicate illustrations.

About the Authors

Dr. Alvin Silverstein is a professor of biology at the College of Staten Island of the City University of New York. **Virginia B. Silverstein** is a translator of Russian scientific literature. The Silversteins first worked together on a research project at the University of Pennsylvania. Since then, they have produced 6 children and more than 170 published books for young people.

Laura Silverstein Nunn, a graduate of Kean College, has been helping with her parents' books since her high school days. She is the coauthor of more than fifty books on diseases and health, science concepts, endangered species, and pets. Laura lives with her husband Matt and their young son Cory in a rural New Jersey town not far from her childhood home.